Missing Pieces

DOROTHY SCOTT

ISBN: 978-1-7321048-0-8
ISBN-13:7321048-0-8

DEDICATION

This book is dedicated to my children
Tanivea Antoinette, LaVall DeShawn
DeMarcus Latrell & DeSean Amari
Whom I love dearly.

CONTENTS

CONTENTS CONT.,

BESTFRIEND

I have been looking for you for years

I thought I found you once but that was so unclear

My best friend knows my name, knows what I'm thinking before I say it

My best friend knows that I'm happy with him and I'm happy without him.

Why is it so hard to find my best friend, we said we would find each other soon?

It's been 42 years and still no you.

I longed to have you around to tell you everything that's going on

What makes me mad, what makes me glad and what keeps me up all night

There came one who looked like you, but he was counterfeit

He was not the real deal but wanted to look like you, smell like you and sound like you

It was all a game to him but not for me, because a broken heart is now me.

Best friend, best friend let's go skating, let's go on a road trip and get to know each other.

Walk with me, talk with me, hold my hand and believe with me.

Oh, how I have searched this world for you, as said before many have come but doesn't look like you.

I'm ready when you are as we have the same hiding place.

I will know you when I see you, so why have you been hidden from me.

I'm ready now, no more heartache, no more pain just thoughts of you soon to be here.

Today it's clear my best friend will soon appear

I will be ready, and my mind is clear

My love for you has always been near

Just come now, come here.

COMPLICATED ORDER

I need love, a listening ear and a quiet soul

I need hugs for no reason and just because gifts

Be still, don't talk, just listen and you can hear my spirit speak

Kisses of affection keeps my heart happy

Consistency keeps jealousy far from me.

Love and affection is what the doctor ordered

Foot rubs and back massages relax my mind body and soul

To know me is to read my mind

My kids have my heart and God is my first love

Be my strength in time of weakness

Hold my hand when fear tries to creep in

Walk alongside me when I feel alone

When critics criticize help build my confidence

When I doubt be my reassurance

It's hard to be me so I will not be another

Take me as I am, and God makes the changes

Together means power alone were scattered

I'm not needy just a complicated order.

SUNSHYNE

I will still shine

When I heard you call me Sunshine

I wasn't sure if I was okay with it, but I smiled

For the first time someone saw the real me

They saw past my hurt, my pain and didn't want anything from me

I had to grow into the name

I didn't understand the reason behind the name

It wasn't until I got older that I realized why you called me sunshine

It was a character builder for me

So many have tried to dim my light

My sun still shined in the midst of the darkness

Even if I didn't want to shine

It was never up to me

God ordained doesn't change because I say no

It comes out everywhere I go.

I changed the spelling to fit me I am Sunshyne with a "Y"

There is only one me

I'm happy with who God made me to be

I will continue to shyne daily.

WILDFLOWER

Wildflowers do grow

Wildflowers are useful to nature

Wildflowers are beautiful too

Put me in a box and I will outgrow it

Put me in a cubicle and I will outgrow it too

Wildflowers grow

Everyone likes tulips and roses

But wildflowers are colorful and multifaceted.

Wildflowers are different shapes and sizes

They're not limited to one area but wildflowers; they still grow

Wildflowers don't always know where they belong

Because they're so different as they grow

Wildflowers don't realize how naturally beautiful they are

The uncertainty of a wildflower helps groom their growth

This keeps them pushing further then where they are now, but they still grow

Don't ever step on a wildflower

Help them grow, they're very useful

Imagine a field of wildflowers different colors and shapes

They make any garden look beautiful

No matter where you put a wildflower they will outgrow that area

Only a wildflower can stop its own growth.

SUPERSTAR

I was made to shine
Everywhere I go
Everything I do
I was made to shine.

If I'm not shining, my spirit is weak
If my spirit is weak, I'm hurting
If I'm hurting, God is not in control
That means I'm trying to do it on my own
I was made to shine.

Only superstars shine in a dark place
My spirit speaks volume
Not my clothing
Not my money
And definitely not my body

Superstars have character
Superstars have confidence
Superstars have competence
And superstars have chemistry

God works out all these features
God works for me
He makes me who I am today
I am a SUPERSTAR!

SOUL TIE

You were tied to my soul in error

God did not ordain for you to be here

Why did I allow this to be a choice for my life?

This was so dark for me and set me back for a season

My heart was broken because I allowed you in my spirit

You looked like the one for me, it was a lie

A wolf in sheep's clothing, it was like looking in a mirror

I knew it was wrong, but it was too late

You laughed at my downfall

I hear you saying I finally got her.

You told me I shouldn't have bitten the apple and I kept going

A feeling that I couldn't explain, what do I do this has never happened before

My flesh was so happy, but my soul was sick

How do I get rid of this illness that is following me everywhere I go?

You're pulling me and I'm pulling you in the spirit

Believing this will work is deception at its finest

Screaming God take this away please I don't want it anymore

Its killing me; my soul is shriveling up and dying

Lord I need you right now, save me from this wickedness

My soul is tied to a demon that looks like mine.

FAVOR

Favor ain't fair when it comes to God
God works in my favor
God shows me favor
God is on my side
Favor ain't fair when it comes to God

Work out your salvation and God can show you favor also
Don't be mad at my favor
The work I have done in the dark calls for favor on my life
Favor ain't fair when it comes to God

What works for me may not work for you
Obedience is better than sacrifice is what I heard
Be obedient to Gods instructions and favor will follow
Find favor with God and you find favor with man
Favor ain't fair when it comes to God

God uses people and cause people to favor you
People that murmur and complain don't have favor with God
They try to diminish your favor with character assassination
But God is working in your favor keep pushing and keep serving
Favor ain't fair when it comes to God.

IDENTITY

I'm lost
I can't see
I have no clue of who I am
Help me find myself

It's been to long
Will someone tell me who I am
Not what you want me to be
But who God called me to be

Don't be selfish and keep it to yourself
Don't diminish my growth to make you feel good about yourself
You have been put into my life to help me along the way
Please tell me who I am

What am I supposed to be doing for Christ
Don't limit my gift to fulfill your own insecurity
God called you, God called me we're here to help each other
So tell me who I am

Take my life Lord and use it for your glory
I found myself when I allowed Christ and not man to tell me, who I am.

FOCUS

I am an intercessor
And I will not be moved
There are distractions everywhere around me
But I will not be moved

When I pray my mind is all over the place
But I will not be moved
My landlord sold his house and I have to move in with family
I will not be moved

My kids are acting out and getting in trouble at school
But I will not be moved
I got laid off from my job and have limited finances
I will not be moved

There is a storm going on around me that's about to take me down
But I will not be moved
The enemy is after my soul and he doesn't give up
I will not be moved

That same spirit is chasing me down from my past
But I will not be moved
I will remain focus on the task at hand
And as an intercessor I will not be moved!

MANTLE

Something that covers, enfolds or envelops

Figurative cloak symbolizing preeminence or authority (Webster's Dictionary)

Prayer is my mantle

Given to me by God

What is birthed in the spirit can't be taken back

Pray, intercede and stand in the gap

Put your own needs last

Pray for the needs of others

Push your plate away

Get an answer from heaven

Wait for a release

Be available all hours of the day

Speak in tongues

Write what you hear and see

Pray it through

Pray for understanding

Release only what you're supposed to release

Timing is everything

Prayer is my mantle and can't be changed.

HELPMATE

I love the Teamwork
I love the Comradery
I love being married
When it's the right person
Being a helpmate is my challenge
I have no idea what I'm doing

The obstacles to overcome together makes it stronger
I am his peace
He is my strength
He is alpha male
I am alpha female
We understand each other

He tells me his vision
I pray it through and watch it manifest right before our eyes
I make sure he has everything he needs to be a provider
I pray with him
I serve God with him

I'm his best friend
I'm his wife
I'm his helpmate
With the help of the holy spirit.

FREE

Freedom is beautiful
It's refreshing
It's life giving
Free from bondage
Free from my past

Freedom is God
Free to be me
Free to live life
I'm so free
I will not go back no matter what

Freedom is my daily bread
I live life on purpose
I embrace freedom
Give my past a wave goodbye
God has set me free

Freedom is my new name
I love
I laugh
I live
I am free!!

EXPRESSION

Express myself
How is that possible
I don't know how
Say how you feel
That is uncomfortable to me

It sounds weird coming out of my mouth
So much of my expression has been in my mind
So how do I get it to come out of my mouth
Some people dance, some people sing, and some may even speak
For me I express myself through writing

This is how God made me
I'm okay with it
This works for me
There's nothing wrong with my expression
I just didn't understand

I express myself to get out how I feel
I express myself to help people understand my person
Uncommon for the common.
Expression.

DEAR MAMA

I thank you for letting the lord use you

It's better than letting the world use you

Thank you for not giving up even though you took a beating on my behalf;

When I got pregnant you still tried to cover me

Thank you.

I know you protected me from those men that wanted me because I look like you.

Thank you for covering me.

I appreciate you for not giving up and leaving your children.

Were all grown now with our own kids (your grandkids) and we know how to teach them

When it gets rough, just keep going, it will get better, press through and don't give up

I love you momma, I thank God for you...

FAMILIAR LOVE

I know it was this love, a familiar love that I would look for from people

I know as a child I experienced this before

No one could measure up to this love that I was looking for.

I would look for love in different men I thought whoever could make me feel like this familiar love that I looked for and craved for then that's who would be with me.

It didn't happen like that because no man, woman or child can measure up to this familiar love that I once knew, I was in love with God and didn't know it.

I searched for years for this familiar love in man after man

It wasn't until I finally heard my love call my name and then I was like it's you! it's you!

Where have you been, I've been looking for you, I was starting to think there was no hope for you and me, once you called my name I knew you were still with me

I just couldn't hear him with all the voices from this world and my own voice in my head

He couldn't come to me with all the mess I was in, looking for God in the eyes of men, women and children and looking for God in sex, drugs and alcohol.

It's a familiar love once felt and experienced and manifested in my life and yours too just open your ears to hear him call you, oh what a relief it is to hear my love call my name.

When I am at my lowest point in depression and can't really hear anyone else but God "My familiar love".

GIVING UP IS HARD TO DO

I just want to stop and give up, to just say I quit, I don't want to be here anymore

I know that's impossible because of my mom.

I would always say my mom didn't teach me anything because she didn't talk to me about life.

She would get drunk and go off at the mouth, babbling and never teaching.

I didn't know what was true or false but once she passed away it wasn't until my brother said it best "my mom raised us to be strong" So lord that's why I can't give up, it's not in me.

I don't care what my mom went through the beatings, the fights, the evictions, the prostitution, the sex, the lies, the suicide attempts, the lust, the drinking the drugs and the poverty.

She still woke up every morning she never gave up, so I couldn't give up if I wanted to.

That's what she taught me how to be strong and never give up without the words coming out of her mouth.

I was supposed to go and talk with her to let her know I wasn't mad at her anymore.

I really wanted to hear her story, just so she could tell someone, I believe I could handle it this time

I had to say with my mouth, "I release my mom to you Lord,"

Saturday afternoon she passed away.

For me giving up is hard to do.

WHERE TO GO FROM HERE

Where do I go next lord?

I've prayed, I've fasted, I'm just glad I woke up this morning

I seem to always say lord I don't want anything else as long as I have you.

Lord I need things and I want things I want the house and the business that you showed me.

So where to next?

Is this my new level already, is it here or is it coming?

I get up every morning and just thank God I'm alive to go to a job

I know that it's not what I want to do but the lord says this is where you belong right now.

At a place I go to sleep knowing that's not where I don't want to be, but the lord says this is where you belong right now.

I come from a place in my life where I don't know anything, when I say lost I mean lost

As a little girl knowing no one loves you or cares for you is hard

As a teenager knowing no one cares or loves you is also hard

Until you give birth to a baby, a girl; only to have to teach her things you have no clue about.

No one told you or taught you, I have to go on instincts or shall I say the grace of God.

Lord don't get me wrong I'm not complaining I am thankful.

Sometimes it doesn't matter if you can't or don't know how to give love back or too afraid.

It all boils down to, "I don't know who I am" or where to go to next and it's scary sometimes.

I know I still have a lot of growing to do but my question to you lord.

Does this mean I still don't trust you?

If so how can I expect something from you; lord right now my desire is to build my relationship

with you, so I can have a relationship with my family and stop just living and just getting by.

I'm tired lord of feeling empty wondering if something is going to change today, even if I

haven't done anything to help my change,

So where do I go from here?

LOVE

The love that I'm too scared to give

I'm afraid it won't be the right love

What is the right love, pure clean godly love

Love from the heart love comes naturally

Love comes softly not the hard love that I lived with for years

Not the abused love that I endured for years

Not the love that left me lonely

No not that love, just pure Agape Love.

THE CHURCH

My prayer for the church is that we will all stand

Stand on your word and stand in your spirit, just stand.

My prayer for the pastor is that he will continue to lead the flock without any hindrance

I pray that he will prosper in his relationship with you father

I rebuke the devour for his name sake, I rebuke every hindrance, confusion, compromise,

unnecessary phone calls, chronic counselees, fatigue, sleepiness and compulsions in Jesus name.

I pray father you will give him a desire and a place to pray in the name of Jesus.

I pray for his wife that she will continue to prosper in her relationship with you,

I pray also father that you will continue to speak into her life by your spirit on a new level.

I pray for prosperity in their marriage and that every need will be met

I rebuke rebellion that may try to come against their children in Jesus name.

HUSBAND

The heavens roared

There was a rustling sound

Then a rumbling

A loud thump

There goes a bang and a boom

The clouds rolled away and sent me you.

You're not perfect

You're just perfect for me

Brown eyes, full lips

Handsome and fresh face

Strong 'cepts

Tall stature.

I knew it was you

Who came in the form of a friend to be with me until the end.

EXAMPLE OF CHRIST

Pray!!!

Pray that the power of the enemy will be broken off his life,

Pray that he will stand firm with his feet shod with the preparation of the gospel of peace.

Pray that every negative soul tie is broken, then rebuke every addiction

Pray that God would help him recognize the work of the enemy

Pray that knowledge and wisdom will come upon his life

Pray that the old mindsets are broken off his life

When you think it's time to relax as a woman because your husband has your back and he's going to cover the family; you get disappointed because he seems to still fall back in some areas.

You realize you still need to pray even if he's in line with the word or whether he's still lacking the word, you still have to pray!

As a woman, you'd like to be able to say, "I can relax now" and thank God my husband has my back.

You really can't relax you still need to pray, if all else fails pray, because he's not going to pray for himself.

Then you start to question God when is it going to be my turn to prosper?

And God answers when you pray!

Pray without ceasing

Pray with wisdom

Pray with knowledge and understanding

Pray without fear

Pray with clarity and most of all pray with power

So you can see an example of Christ on Earth.

CLEAN HOUSE

I understand now a garnished house is only possible through your grace

It can't be done on my own

I know that I am your temple and it's a sacred place

I am to treat it as such

I thank God for the truth that's in me

Truth is love, truth is not to hurt us

we are not capable of truth on our own.

Defiled denied: it's not what goes in our mouth that makes us unclean

It's what comes out that makes us unclean.

With my new heart I serve you

The old one cannot work in the new kingdom

I know before I see you I am to approach you ready and willing

Purified and clean even if it takes months or years

I come to you with no blemishes or scars

Knowing you heal and bind all wounds from the past

As a radiant woman, my work is now done, it's up to me to follow you

Your will for me is to remain Holy as you are Holy.

I am now clean and made new.

MISSING PIECE

There is still something missing

I have everything I need

God is good to me

Business is good

Finances are in order

There is something missing

My life is in order according to the word of God

My kids are happy and living life as they should

I serve my church and my community

There's just something missing and that something is you

Come out of hiding so we can find each other; my missing piece.

ABOUT THE AUTHOR

Dorothy is first and foremost an avid reader.

Reading became an escape for her at an early age. Until she discovered she could write.

Years later writing became her escape.

Dorothy is now a budding entrepreneur and working on her upcoming business ventures.

She loves road trips and beautiful scenery.

She resides in San Antonio, Texas with her four children.

This is her first book, but will definitely not be her last.

www.ingramcontent.com/pod-product-compliance
Lightning Source LLC
Chambersburg PA
CBHW070113070426
42448CB00038B/2619